DISCARD

SPACE TOURISM

WRITTEN BY **Peter McMahon**
ILLUSTRATED BY **Andy Mora**

Kids Can Press

To my sweet wife, Kristina, and to Cynnie and Honey for their constant support and for serving as my role models for being a tourist — P.M.

Acknowledgments

Andy and I had an especially fun time making this book in the series, just as the first suborbital tourists were getting ready for their maiden space vacations. Many thanks to all the people who made this book possible, including Brian Binnie, Anousheh Ansari, Suni Williams, the folks at escience.ca and John Spencer, who has been invaluable in acquainting me with the people who are pioneering space tourism today and tomorrow. Thanks to my good friend and experiment collaborator, David Howard. Finally, thanks again to my editor Karen Li for putting up with me for another book!

Kids Can Press acknowledges the financial support of the Government of Ontario, through the Ontario Media Development Corporation's Ontario Book Initiative; the Ontario Arts Council; the Canada Council for the Arts; and the Government of Canada, through the BPIDP, for our publishing activity.

Published in Canada by
Kids Can Press Ltd.
25 Dockside Drive
Toronto, ON M5A 0B5

Published in the U.S. by
Kids Can Press Ltd.
2250 Military Road
Tonawanda, NY 14150

www.kidscanpress.com

Edited by Karen Li
Designed by Julia Naimska

This book is smyth sewn casebound.
Manufactured in Singapore, in 3/2011 by Tien Wah Press (Pte) Ltd.

CM 11 0 9 8 7 6 5 4 3 2 1

Library and Archives Canada Cataloguing in Publication

McMahon, Peter, 1977–
    Space tourism / written by Peter McMahon ; illustrated by Andy Mora.

(Machines of the future)
Includes index.
ISBN 978-1-55453-368-8

1. Space vehicles — Juvenile literature. 2. Space tourism — Juvenile literature. I. Mora, Andy II. Title. III. Series: Machines of the future

TL793.M35 2011   j629.47   C2011-900087-3

Kids Can Press is a *lorus*™ Entertainment company

4/18

Contents

GO INTO SPACE TODAY!

What if you could blast off in a rocket and travel thousands of kilometers (miles) an hour? Imagine playing your favorite sport while floating in slow motion, or drinking water by drifting toward a droplet suspended in midair, or taking a space walk with nothing but a 5 mm (1/4 in.) spacesuit between you and the cosmos …

What if you could do all those things right now?

When we humans first set our sights on space travel, only a handful of pilots were chosen to go. Each trip was extremely dangerous and required years of training. Many of the first rockets failed to ignite, blew up in midair or caught on fire, never having left the launchpad. Aircraft test pilots of the 1950s often paid for the ride with their lives, and rocket men of the 1960s faced even more explosive risks.

After a series of remote-controlled launches in the U.S. and Russia (many of which ended in flames of the wrong kind), the first piloted space capsules successfully made it into space for a few minutes, then into orbit around Earth for a few hours. Eventually, some of the people who flew in these tiny pods sealed their helmets shut and pressurized their spacesuits to float outside for a few minutes: the first space walks.

Later versions of these tiny spaceships held two or more astronauts. By modifying these pods for longer stays, space explorers could live in these temporary habitats for weeks at a time. This was also the beginning of experiments in space. While traveling in these vehicles astronauts could research how our bodies react to low-gravity environments.

During the 1960s and '70s, humans landed on the Moon (six times!) by using huge skyscraper-sized rockets. We built and lived on the first space stations and sent robot probes to Venus, Mars, Jupiter and Saturn. We also launched satellites and other objects into orbit, as well as hundreds of rockets.

In this age before international cooperation in space, each country developed its own specialties: The U.S. mastered building spaceships to other worlds (such as the Apollo Moon rockets, the Viking Mars landers and the Voyager probes that explored most of the outer solar system). Meanwhile, space scientists and engineers in Russia became experts at building space stations.

The 1980s saw the blastoff of NASA's space shuttles, the first reusable spaceships that astronauts could use to launch large satellites, live in space for more than a week and conduct science experiments from. These futuristic-looking space planes could house a crew of up to seven highly trained experts for some of the most difficult expeditions in history. At the same time, we sent robot spaceships to Neptune and Uranus and built Mir, the first full-scale research outpost in orbit.

But nowadays, space travel isn't just for professional astronauts doing research or orbital engineers building space stations. It's for people like you … and it could be a lot of fun.

Even as you read this book, tickets for trips into space are already on sale. Zero-gravity (zero-g) simulators have let thousands of people hover in midair, just like astronauts. Rocket-powered planes are soaring into the blackness of space. There's even a

space hotel getting ready to open in Earth orbit.

How would you like to take your next family vacation in zero gravity? Read on, and get ready to punch-it into the final frontier!

A HISTORY OF SPACE TOURISM, PART 1: TRIPS FOR THE RICH

You could say that Russia's Yuri Gagarin paved the way for your upcoming trip into space. Gagarin, a Russian fighter pilot, became the first human to leave Earth and soar past the clouds into space. It was 1961, and no one knew what to expect. In an hour and a half, Gagarin flew around our planet at an altitude of 327 km (203 mi.) in his tiny Vostok I capsule. He then ejected 7 km (4 mi.) above the ground and landed by parachute.

Space tour trivia

Many of the first space tourists prefer not to be called tourists. They say that the rigorous selection process, multimonth training sessions and potential dangers make public space travel less like a trip to a theme park and more like an expedition to scale Mount Everest. True space tourism, they say, will involve less training and a lot more people.

Since Gagarin's safe return to Earth, hundreds of astronauts have followed in his footsteps, piloting orbiting capsules, reusable space planes, rockets to the Moon and space stations.

It was on the largest of those early outposts — the Russian space station Mir — that Toyohiro Akiyama almost became the first space tourist: In 1990, the Japanese television news reporter got to orbit Earth for a week on Mir. But because he was working and not on vacation (his company, a Japanese television station, paid for the trip), he doesn't quite count as the first space tourist.

More than 10 years later, American businessman Dennis Tito claimed the title of "first space tourist" by buying a ticket for a Russian Soyuz capsule. After training for several months, Tito rocketed to the International Space Station (ISS), where he spent nearly eight days in orbit. The price tag? US$20 million. While in orbit at the ISS, Tito experienced weightlessness, ate prepackaged food with NASA and Russian crew members, photographed Earth from space and conducted science experiments.

In the years that followed, close to a dozen paying customers orbited Earth and lived in space. Anousheh Ansari, the first female space tourist, blasted off in 2006. She also became the first tourist to write a blog from space. Charles Simonyi became the first person to take two vacations in space. His first trip was in 2007, and his second was in 2009.

As cool as all this was, though, space tourism remained a millionaire's game. News reports claimed that Simonyi paid US$25 million for his first voyage into space.

Space adventures here on Earth

Back on solid ground, you can simulate your own trip into space on your computer, using free 3-D software that lets you fly through a photorealistic universe, complete with planets, stars and galaxies. Such software ranges from Microsoft's WorldWide Telescope and Google Sky (both free) to the beautifully realistic Starry Night, which costs around US$80 and reproduces photorealistic horizons from country and city settings and even lets you add your own horizons.

LIVING ON THE INTERNATIONAL SPACE STATION

The International Space Station is the biggest space structure ever built. With 16 contributing countries, it is the largest multinational engineering project of all time. Spanning 109 m (358 ft.) by 73 m (240 ft.), the 400 tonne (441 ton) vehicle is larger than an entire soccer field. Look up at the right place and time on a clear night and you may see it soaring overhead, often appearing as the brightest "star" in the sky.

Space tour trivia

Space food used to be gross. It was mostly dehydrated (all the water removed) and then had to be rehydrated, or it was pureed into goo that had to be squeezed from tubes like those you find toothpaste in. Today, the crews of the International Space Station have tasted fresh-from-frozen space meals designed by celebrity chefs Wolfgang Puck and Rachael Ray.

One of the ISS's roles is that of a research outpost for professional astronauts: researchers, engineers and other mission specialists. It's also a test bed for technologies to be used on longer-term space trips beyond Earth orbit. When the Russian government and an American tourism company started offering tickets to the public to fly to the ISS in 2001, part of the orbital lab also became the first space hotel.

So how does a stay at the ISS compare to a night in a hotel on Earth? First of all, most of the modules on the ISS are about a quarter the size of a small Earth hotel room. Second, remember those Maximum Occupancy signs in hotel rooms? The ISS has a similar rule for its inhabitants. The maximum number of people on the space station is limited by the number of seats available in the emergency escape craft. On the ISS, there are six available seats in two Russian Soyuz capsules. Third, there's a lot more than a bed, a table and a lamp in your living space on the ISS. Each module is crammed with things such as computers, storage containers, exercise equipment, tools for experiments and machinery to help keep the station in working order. It may all be worth it for the view, but let's hope that future space hotels will at least feature bathrooms larger than a refrigerator. (That's about the size of the one on the ISS.)

Once onboard the ISS, paying space tourists aren't expected to pitch in on the daily maintenance of the station or conduct experiments, though most vacationers tend to do so to get the full experience of being an astronaut.

While on the ISS, many space tourists conduct scientific research of their own design or experiments that others request they try. In the future, those chores could be replaced by more vacation-style experiences involving zero-g sports and other forms of entertainment.

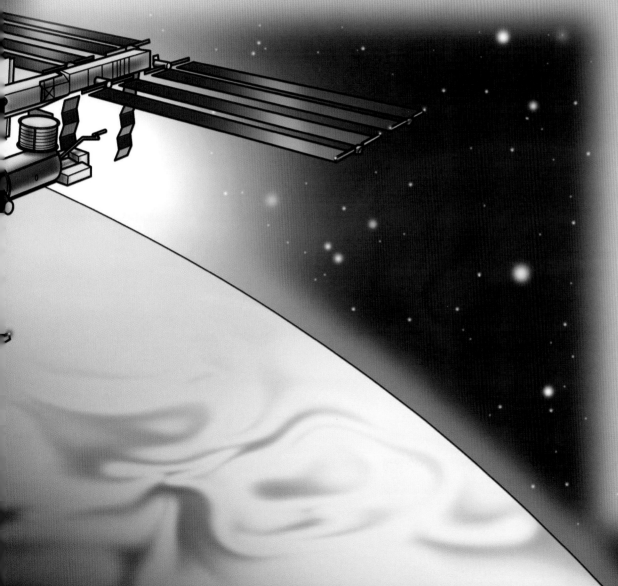

ROCKET SCIENCE 101:
WHAT IS GRAVITY?

One of the first challenges for spacecraft engineers was to build ships that could overcome Earth's gravity. Gravity attracts objects to each other: The more mass an object has, the stronger the attraction to that object.

The force of gravity is especially visible when one object (let's say, you) gets together with an object of much larger mass (say, Earth). Because Earth's mass is more than yours, you are pulled toward Earth. In much the same way, our more massive Sun keeps Earth and all the other planets in orbit.

To overcome Earth's gravity and enter into orbit around our planet, spacecraft have to reach a speed of approximately 24 000 km/h (15 000 m.p.h.). Astronauts accelerating to this speed in a spaceship temporarily experience several times the normal gravity we usually feel on Earth. To escape Earth's gravitational influence (such as on a trip to the Moon), you need to get up to 40 000 km/h (25 000 m.p.h.) or about 11 km (7 mi.) per second.

Life as a satellite

If you were an astronaut floating in space, gravity would tend to pull you toward your spaceship — but not as much as you, your spaceship, the Moon and all nearby satellites are being pulled toward the much more massive Earth.

Earth's gravity keeps our Moon and human-made satellites in orbit. But did you know that the Moon is large enough and far enough that it's slowly drifting away? On the contrary, human-made satellites and spacecraft are small enough and close enough that they are all slowly drifting toward Earth. Spacecraft and satellites often solve this problem by using maneuvering thrusters to constantly "boost" themselves back into orbit.

PROJECT #1: PENCIL ERASER GRAVITY SIMULATOR

The pull of gravity is already acting on you and everything around you. But you can also simulate the effects of gravity right here on Earth. Just grab a few household materials and amaze all those around you with this handy experiment. It mimics how astronaut and space tourism facilities simulate different degrees of gravity during training.

YOU WILL NEED

a square of heavy cardboard, approximately 10 cm x 10 cm (4 in. x 4 in.)

1 to 2 m (3 to 6 ft.) of string

an eraser

scissors

Expert Interview

"You adjust to everything eventually, but the g-forces during liftoff are more intense than anything else during the mission, except for the vibrations you feel when the solid rocket boosters fire. My crewmates told me to remember to breathe out during the launch ... which I did, most of the time. Having said that, imagine you were the tiny eraser in the experiment in this book at the beginning of a space launch!"
— NASA astronaut Sunita Williams, whose 2007 flight was the longest mission of any woman in history

INSTRUCTIONS

1 Using the scissors, carefully poke a small hole in each of the four corners of the cardboard.

2 Cut the string into four equal lengths. Tie the end of each length to one of the four corners of the cardboard. Ask someone to hold the cardboard down on a level surface. Then pull the four strings up until taut. Tie the ends together.

3 Place the eraser in the middle of the square of cardboard: When you tip the cardboard on its side, the eraser should slide off.

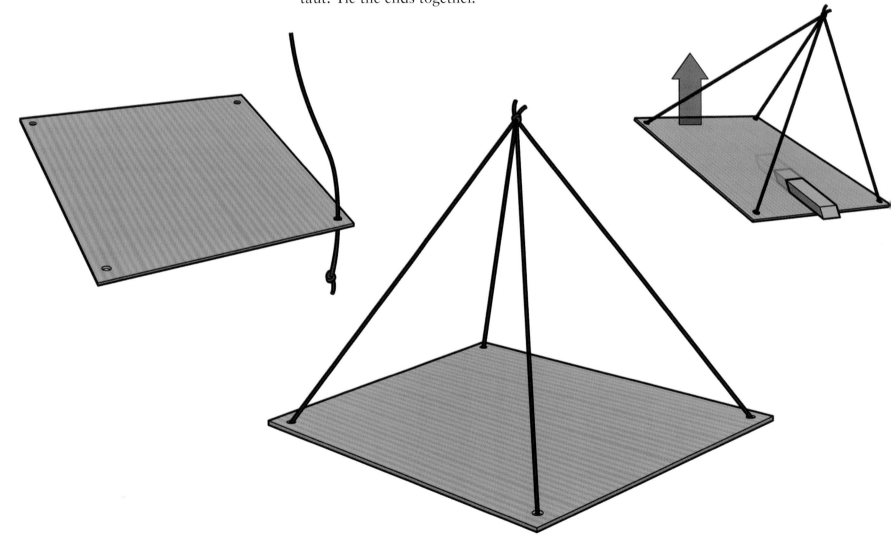

4 In a large room (without any breakable objects) or outside, place the eraser in the middle of the square of cardboard. Then grasp the knotted ends of the strings so that the cardboard platform hangs in midair. Keep the eraser level.

5 Slowly start to swing the platform around in a circle. Gradually increase its speed until you can swing it overhead with the eraser still "onboard."

Your eraser is "plastered" to the cardboard platform in this simulation of gravitational force called a centrifuge. This is a small-scale version of the simulators that space agencies and fighter jet schools use. Simulators show test subjects how high levels of gravity will feel without having to blast off for real.

A HISTORY OF SPACE TOURISM, PART 2: SPACE TRIPS FOR ALL!

In 2004, space tourism changed from a sport for the ultrarich to something that more people would be able to afford. That October, *SpaceShipOne* — a test space plane — became the first working vehicle specially built to take paying customers into suborbit.

NASA's space shuttles use 46 m (151 ft.) tall rocket boosters and engines powered by office building–sized liquid fuel tanks to push off from Earth. They blast off with the equivalent of more than a million horsepower. By comparison, *SpaceShipOne* is quietly

lifted halfway to maximum altitude under a booster plane. The space plane then detaches and fires a rocket system about the size of a minivan to get its passengers the rest of the way.

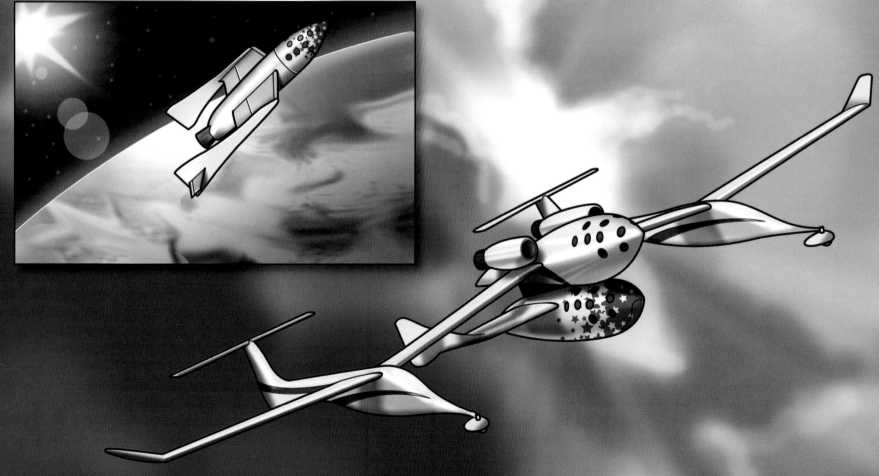

SpaceShipOne was built by Scaled Composites, an aerospace company that also built *GlobalFlyer*, the record holder for the fastest aircraft flight around the world on a single tank of fuel. *SpaceShipOne* was designed to win the US$10 million Ansari X Prize. The competition challenged companies to build a vehicle that could voyage into space — at least 100 km (62 mi.) above the surface of Earth — twice in two weeks. On October 4, 2004, with test pilot Brian Binnie at the controls, *SpaceShipOne* made history, officially claiming the X Prize. That year, *SpaceShipOne* and its booster plane, *White Knight*, made more flights than NASA's space shuttles typically make in a year.

After the X Prize win, *SpaceShipOne* was placed in Washington, DC's National Air and Space Museum. Scaled Composites founder Burt Rutan then created The Spaceship Company to build the larger *SpaceShipTwo*. You can already book a trip on a version of *SpaceShipTwo* for about US$200 000 dollars, or about the price of a small house!

Space Race

SpaceShipOne and *SpaceShipTwo* differ from NASA's space shuttles in size, range and complexity: NASA's space shuttles have often been referred to as the most complex machines on Earth. By contrast, *SpaceShipOne* and *SpaceShipTwo* are models of simplicity. However, since the space shuttles fly high into orbit and *SpaceShipOne* and *SpaceShipTwo* go only up and straight back down, comparing these spacecrafts is fun but not totally fair:

	NASA space shuttles	*SpaceShipOne* and *SpaceShipTwo*
Building cost	Space shuttle *Endeavour* cost just under US$2 billion.	*SpaceShipOne* cost US$40 million (50 times cheaper than the cost of building a space shuttle).
Crew capacity	NASA's space shuttles can carry up to seven crew members and several tonnes of cargo.	*SpaceShipOne* has a crew of one. *SpaceShipTwo* can carry two crew members and up to six passengers.
Distance capability	Space shuttles can soar as high as 530 km (330 mi.) above Earth to orbit stably.	*SpaceShipOne* and *SpaceShipTwo* can fly more than 100 km (62 mi.) into space for a few minutes.

ROCKET SCIENCE 101:
WHAT IS ZERO GRAVITY?

The view of Earth from afar is amazing. But there's another thing that rocks about being in space: the sense of weightlessness. So what causes it? And does space really make you weightless?

First, let's take a closer look at what gives things weight on Earth. More than 300 years ago, British scientist Isaac Newton wondered why apples fell down from trees. (Why didn't they fall left or right or up into the air?) Newton proposed that every object was subject to a force called gravity. According to Newton, anything with mass (or molecules, the stuff of matter) attracts objects toward it and is attracted to other objects itself.

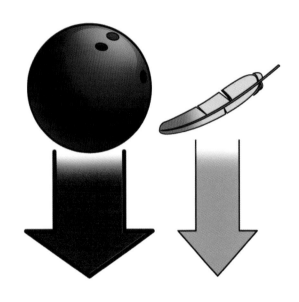

The more mass an object has, the more it will pull on things. Earth pulls on every object on or near it because it is more massive than all those objects.

A massive object like a bowling ball will be pulled toward Earth with more force than something less massive, like a feather. In this way, the bowling ball weighs more than the feather on Earth. But in space, away from Earth's gravity, neither the bowling ball nor the feather weigh anything at all, even though both still have mass (and the bowling ball has more mass than the feather).

Astronauts often refer to this as microgravity instead of the more famous zero gravity. In true interstellar space, far from any nearby stars like our Sun, you could float forever in zero gravity. But throughout interplanetary space — around planets like Earth — there's still a little bit of gravity, called microgravity. In a spaceship, you can float around and toss objects such as pens and food into the air and see them drift for minutes. But sooner or later, everything will settle on the "ground" — the surface facing Earth.

Expert Interview

"The most interesting thing about being in space is that you don't notice what is a wall or what is a floor: Sometimes you notice that you have, say, a laptop anchored to the ceiling … As soon as you stand up, it clicks in your head — the room switches, and you distinctly feel that switch instantly."
— Anousheh Ansari, first female space tourist and first private space blogger

PROJECT #2: ZERO-G IN A LAUNDRY BASKET

Space agencies and space tourism companies simulate microgravity by flying a special plane in a series of steep climbs and dives (called parabolas). At the top of the climb and before the plane begins to dive, everyone inside the plane experiences the rush of weightlessness.

But who needs an airplane to simulate weightlessness? You can do it in this next experiment with a few basement-variety items.

YOU WILL NEED

1 m (3 ft.) of thread

a sewing needle as long as a table tennis ball is wide

a table tennis ball

a laundry basket (preferably with holes in the sides)

a second laundry basket (optional)

a small, light digital camera with the ability to record video (optional)

a marker (optional)

scissors (optional)

masking tape (optional)

Expert Interview

"It's really hard to get used to doing everything more gently than on Earth: I actually hit my head a few times because I was used to applying a certain amount of force to get somewhere on Earth. The table tennis ball experiment here reminds me of how clumsy you are to start with in microgravity."

— Anousheh Ansari, first female space tourist and first private space blogger

INSTRUCTIONS

1 Thread the sewing needle. Then carefully wiggle the needle in the middle of the table tennis ball until you poke a hole in it. Wiggle the needle around to make the hole a little wider. Then poke the needle through the opposite end of the ball. Again, wiggle the needle around the second hole before pulling the thread all the way through.

2 With the table tennis ball strung halfway along the thread, tie the ends of the thread to opposite sides of one of the laundry baskets. The thread should run parallel to the basket's handles and be tied taut. The ball should be centered inside the basket, halfway between the bottom and the rim of the basket.

3 Now raise the basket over your head (the ball will slide to one end of the thread) and quickly lower it to your feet. The ball, which was resting on the side of the basket, should "float" toward the opposite side of the basket. Every time you do this, you are mimicking the simulated zero gravity of an airplane flying "roller coaster" parabolas. For a moment, your table tennis ball (just like people in the parabola-plane) is "weightless."

4 Optional: If you have a digital camera that can record video, center its lens on the underside of the second laundry basket and carefully trace the camera's outline with the marker (being sure not to get marker on the camera). Also draw in the placement and size of the camera lens.

5 Using the scissors, cut a hole in the bottom of the second laundry basket for the camera lens. Then cut a hole near the top and bottom of each side of the outline.

6 Place the camera back against the underside of the basket, with the lens facing into the basket. Then secure the camera by threading masking tape through the holes at the corners of the outline and taping the camera tight against the basket. Finally, tape the two laundry baskets together at the rims.

7 Press the record button on the camera. Now repeat step 3 and keep recording until you have gotten the table tennis ball to hover for at least a fraction of a second.

You can now play back your experiment to watch the simulated zero gravity you've created. You can even use video editing software to replay your experiment in slow motion, and then you can e-mail the video to your friends and family.

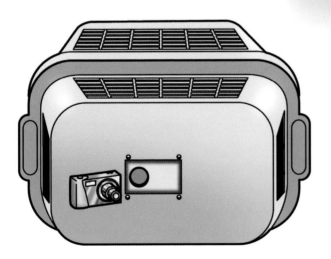

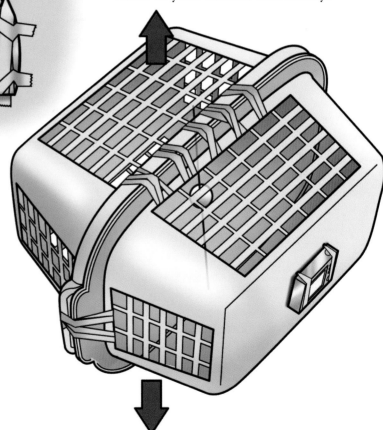

TODAY'S SPACE FLEET

Want to experience the thrill of weightlessness and the view of Earth from orbit now? A hanger full of ships are gearing up to take you into space. Some of them — such as *SpaceShipTwo* — are already flying high. Others are still being tested here on Earth. Here's a look at how some of these ships stack up.

FALCON 9 AND DRAGON

Founded by Elon Musk, cofounder of PayPal, SpaceX was asked by NASA to create an orbital launch vehicle that could help deliver supplies to the ISS. The result was the *Falcon 9* rocket. In 2010, SpaceX made history: It's *Dragon* capsule became the first privately-owned space vehicle to orbit our planet and return to Earth. In the future, *Falcon 9* rockets could carry *Dragon* capsules full of people into Earth orbit.

NEW SHEPARD

Jeff Bezos, owner of the online bookstore Amazon.com, launched the Blue Origin company with the goal of sending customers into space sometime after 2011. Its spaceship — *New Shepard* — is designed to take off and land vertically, like a helicopter or Harrier jet. The craft is designed to carry tourists and researchers up to low suborbital space, meaning altitudes of more than 100 km (62 mi.).

PIXEL

Looking like a cluster of helium balloons, Armadillo Aerospace's *Pixel* rocket is also designed for vertical takeoff and landing. In 2008, *Pixel* won the NASA-sponsored Northrop Grumman Lunar Lander Challenge. As such, Armadillo Aerospace has received funding to build a version of *Pixel* that could one day be a working Moon lander. Armadillo Aerospace plans to enter a new version of *Pixel* in the next Lunar Lander Challenge. To win, it must demonstrate that it can hover and move back-and-forth in midair.

RUSSIAN MIG FIGHTER JET

Right now, for about the cost of a used car, you can take a ride in a Russian MiG fighter jet to "the edge of space," about 20 km (12 mi.) into the stratosphere. Though most space organizations agree that space begins 100 km (62 mi.) above Earth, the MiG will take you high enough to see the curve of Earth. There, the blue haze of our atmosphere gives way to the blackness of space, even in the daytime. Such close-to-space tours cost between US$10 000 and $18 000.

BLACK SKY

Black Sky is a winged rocket plane that could launch tourists into suborbit from several locations in Europe. *Black Sky* is different from other space tourism vehicles because it can be configured to transport either tourists or science experiments for flights that include four to five minutes of weightlessness. *Black Sky* is a creation of Project Enterprise, a German group hoping to have the rocket plane launching on test flights sometime after 2013, with flights for the public several years later.

ROCKET SCIENCE 101:
HOW DO ROCKETS WORK?

As Newton said, for every action, there is an equal and opposite reaction. You can see this when you blow up a balloon and let it go without tying it off. The balloon pushes against the air that rushes out of it. This is the action. At the same time, *the air pushes back against the balloon,* making it speed off in the opposite direction. This is the reaction.

In the same way, the action of rocket propellant erupting out of a rocket causes a reaction that pushes the rocket in the opposite direction of the blast. This works whether the rocket is leaving a launchpad on Earth or blasting out of orbit for the planets.

But a rocket isn't just a gigantic firework. Many rockets channel the explosions created by these chemical reactions through movable nozzles. Directing the explosive flow helps to steer the path of the rocket through the air and through space.

Rocket engines can generally fire in one of two ways:
1. A liquid fuel, such as hydrogen, is exposed to an oxidizer, such as liquid oxygen, to ignite the fuel.
2. A solid rocket motor has the oxidizer embedded in a dry, hard fuel, such as magnesium.

Solid-fuel rockets are stable, durable and more powerful than their liquid fuel–based counterparts, but they can't be turned off once ignited and must be used soon after they are built to keep the fuel from decomposing.

Liquid-fuel rockets can be "throttled" up and down in a controlled way but are more fragile and contain many more parts than solid-fuel rockets. The oxidizer (liquid oxygen) used for liquid-fuel rockets must also be kept cold at all times.

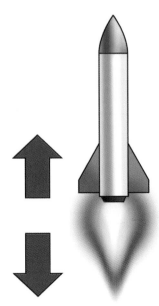

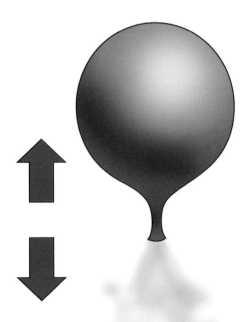

Space tour trivia

Did you know you could laugh your way into space? Okay, that's not totally true. But one of the main ingredients in modern hybrid rocket engines (part solid fuel, part liquid fuel) is nitrous oxide, otherwise known as laughing gas. Nitrous oxide is also used by dentists to numb nerves and by mechanics to increase power output in some racing cars.

PROJECT #3: NEWTON'S BALLOON TEST ENGINE

Many modern spaceships designed for tourism involve two engine stages. The different stages are not stacked one on top of the other like traditional multistage rockets. Instead, space tourism vehicles are more likely to take the form of a large "first stage" plane with a smaller "second stage" space vehicle attached to it. Try this experiment to see up close how a multistage space plane gets going.

YOU WILL NEED

2 chairs

12 m (39 ft.) of fishing line

2 drinking straws

2 long balloons

masking tape

scissors

a friend or family member

Expert Interview

"A thousand things have to happen before a spaceship takes off, and a thousand more before that spaceship and its various stages deliver the astronauts aboard into orbit. Think about that when you watch your multistage balloon rocket take off!"

— Sunita Williams, NASA astronaut and International Space Station crew member

INSTRUCTIONS

1 Place two chairs as far apart as possible. If you can't place them at least 10 m (30 ft.) apart somewhere inside, do this experiment outside.

2 Tie one end of the fishing line to the highest point of one of the chairs. Thread the fishing line through the two straws, and make sure they can slide freely. Then tie the other end of the fishing line to the highest point of the second chair.

3 Blow up one balloon but don't tie it off. Instead, hold the balloon closed while you tape it in one place to the first straw on the line. The straw should lay lengthwise along the top of the balloon.

4 Have your helper keep the first balloon pinched closed while you add a second balloon-and-straw setup to the line. But this time, blow up the second balloon only halfway. (This will simulate the smaller, second-stage space plane.)

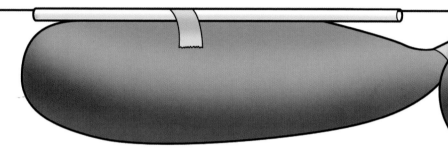

Second Balloon

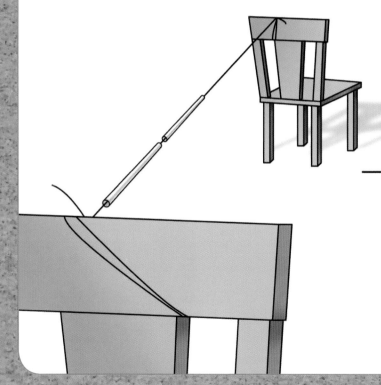

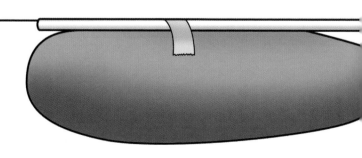

5 With both balloons taped to their straws, push the second balloon up against the first so that the tip of the first balloon blocks the opening of the second balloon from letting air out.

6 Place a strip of masking tape flat across the neck of the second balloon's opening (without covering the opening itself). Then press the tape flat against the tip of the first balloon. When the first balloon deflates, the neck of the second balloon will open.

7 With both balloons at one end of the fishing line, release the opening of the first balloon. BLASTOFF! Does one "stage" fire after the other?

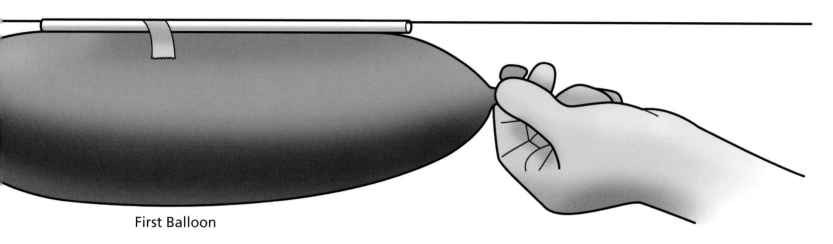

First Balloon

How is this experiment like the space shuttle or moon rockets? The air rushing out of the ends of the balloons provides an action, just like that of ignited fuel being pushed out of the nozzle of a rocket engine. The reaction is your straw-and-balloon spaceship being pushed in the opposite direction, just like a real spaceship. Once the first balloon has deflated, the lack of pressure on the second balloon allows air to rush out of its opening, activating your ship's second stage and propelling it onward!

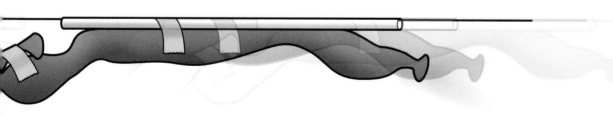

LIFTOFF IN 5 ... 4 ... 3 ... 2 ... 1 ...

Many career astronauts have sat on the launchpad while those fateful numbers counted down. In the case of government vehicles, such as the Russian Soyuz or NASA's space shuttle, the countdown officially would start *days* before liftoff. (That was quite a while for those butterflies in your stomach to hang around.) Routine checks on everything from mechanical parts to sensors to the craft's heat-shield tiles were made and remade by hundreds of people before each launch.

Hours before a space shuttle launch, the huge orange liquid-fuel tank would still be empty. When launch controllers confirmed the weather would allow them to launch, 2 000 000 L (530,000 gal.) of propellant would be pumped into the tank over three hours. A few hours later, the crew would ride a colossal elevator up the launch tower and be strapped into their seats in the shuttle.

Even after they were strapped in, space shuttle astronauts sometimes waited hours more in their seats before the launch began, especially if there was a delay. Just like during a football game, NASA's countdown clock could (and often did) get stopped for additional checks, for bad weather or for technicians to fix any glitches that came up. For long delays, astronauts would be unstrapped and would re-enter the cabin the next possible launch day.

Before a Soyuz launch, news reporters, VIPs and launch staff are allowed right up beside the rocket to talk with the crew at the base of the launch tower elevator. During the Soyuz launch, everyone but the astronauts is hundreds of meters (feet) away. In the case of a space shuttle and next-generation NASA craft, everyone moves many kilometers (miles) away long before the launch. A bus drives the support crew (who strapped in the astronauts) away from the launchpad.

The *really* exciting part of a shuttle launch is once the countdown reaches T-minus one minute (which means one minute before blastoff). At this point, everything starts happening very fast:

- At T-minus 30 seconds, the shuttle switches to internal power instead of being "plugged in" to the launch tower. The computers on the shuttle take over control of the launch from those at Mission Control.
- At T-minus 10 seconds, the shuttle is ready to "go for main engine start," as the launch announcer says.
- At T-minus 6 seconds, the three main shuttle engines start one after the other (about 0.25 seconds apart from each other). They are all controlled by the shuttle's computers. The shuttle rocks forward about a meter (a few feet) as clouds of smoke billow out from underneath it, and the crew hears the thundering roar of the engines from inside the cockpit.

- At T-minus 0, the mighty solid rocket boosters (SRBs) fire with a deafening *KABOOM* that is heard outside but muffled inside the cabin. At the same time, clamps holding down the boosters release, and the shuttle rises into the air atop a cloud of smoke and fire. A launch of such a craft is so spectacular, it often sets off car alarms many kilometers (miles) away.

Expert Interview

"When you're sitting there, it makes everything real. The launch itself happens so quickly: The pressure starts building up, but it doesn't last that long, then after 10 minutes, you're weightless. There's nothing like it. You start feeling light in your feet and start feeling like lifting off your seat. I giggled actually. More than anything, I want to go back and spend more time in space."
— Anousheh Ansari, the world's first female space tourist

The launch of a space tourism vehicle is calm compared with that of a shuttle launch. Smaller engines are used to carry a smaller amount of weight (one to eight people and no cargo) to a much lower altitude. As such, space vacation "launches" will be much smoother than a trip on a Soyuz vehicle or the space shuttle.

In the case of *SpaceShipOne* or *SpaceShipTwo*, a long wait is part of the launch. It takes about an hour for the first-stage carrier plane to lift to an altitude where the rocket in the second stage (the actual space plane) can be fired.

Expert Interview

"You go through such a change between lifting off the runway to firing the rocket lower down in the atmosphere to flying in space. All the controls for *SpaceShipOne* were manual, so during the first test flights, I was controlling it every second with flight stick and pedals. When the motor first lights with a scream, the ship starts bucking like a rodeo bull as you try to steer it through the thundering air. But very quickly, as you get closer to space, the air thins out and the noise dies down. Then, when I'd switch off the rocket engine, things would get totally peaceful almost instantly: The ship starts gliding through the wispier parts of our atmosphere, the vibrations are gone and everything starts floating around. In a way, it's not so different from the working model space plane you can build and launch with the instructions that follow." — Brian Binnie, *SpaceShipOne* test pilot

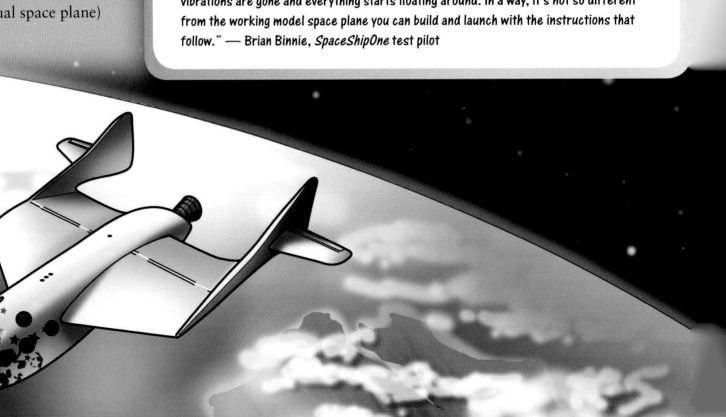

PROJECT #4: LAUNCH A SPACE VACATION PLANE

ONLINE EXLUSIVE!

SpaceShipTwo reaches space by riding under a gigantic carrier plane called *WhiteKnightTwo*. Once *SpaceShipTwo* is carried as far as *WhiteKnightTwo* can go, *SpaceShipTwo* detaches and fires its rocket. When the rocket burns out, *SpaceShipTwo*'s pilots and passengers enjoy the view of Earth from suborbit and several minutes of near-weightlessness before gliding back down to Earth.

While you're saving up the US$200 000 or so it'll take to buy a ticket for *SpaceShipTwo*, you can make a working scale model of a dual-stage space plane. This is a cosmic vacation that can be launched from a field near you. Find the full plans — along with demo images and video — online at **www.kidscanpress.com/ machinesofthefuture**.

YOU WILL NEED

booster plane fin template (online)

a scrap of flat plastic

a 2L (2 qt.) plastic soda pop bottle

duct tape

glue gun

a plastic salad dressing bottle with elongated neck

a broomstick

booster plane nose cone template (online)

bristol board

tape

space plane wing template (online)

space plane stabilizer fin template (online)

two wooden dowels

a variety of coins or metal washers

bicycle pump with hose and valve

Expert Interview

"The time just before a shuttle launch is a fun anticipation for an astronaut, sort of like when you're coming over the top in a roller coaster that you've never been on before. When you get close — six seconds out — it's exciting, but you're also concentrating on your job, so you're distracted from all that fire under the rocket. On my shuttle launch, there was a lot of noise and a LOT of vibration. When my sister saw my launch, she said 'OMG, I couldn't believe there was so much fire.' You can get a sense of what it's like to wait and then feel the exhilaration of liftoff when launching your own two-stage rocket in the plans that start in this book and continue online." — NASA astronaut Sunita Williams, whose 2007 flight was the longest mission of any woman in history

GREEN SPACE TOURISM

Could space tourism become a kind of ecotourism? By all accounts, everyone who has seen our planet from space falls in love with it and feels a strong duty to protect it when back on solid ground. But so far, we humans have made our share of space garbage. Experts estimate there are as many as 500 000 pieces of "space junk," ranging from screws to rocket stages, floating around in Earth orbit. About 20 000 of those pieces are larger than a baseball.

You could say the original attempts at green spacecrafts were the space shuttles. They were conceived in the 1960s and '70s to be the world's first reusable spaceships. The shuttles themselves were used flight after flight. The solid rocket boosters were also used for more than one mission. Only the liquid-fuel tank was junked each launch, when it was jettisoned to burn up in Earth's atmosphere.

Twenty-first century space tourism ships often use smaller rockets than traditional spacecraft because they are carried partway into space by giant carrier planes. This reduces the amount of pollution created by burning fuel. When possible, *SpaceShipOne* and *SpaceShipTwo* use propellant made from biofuels, and all

components of these launch vehicles can be used over and over again.

People on future extended-stay space tourism craft and space hotels will be forced to live green — much more so than in most hotels on Earth. All water will have to be recycled, and waste will be kept to a minimum to be transported back to Earth for recycling or safe disposal. There just isn't a lot of space in space to store things such as garbage and wastewater.

Crews on the International Space Station are already "living green" to a large extent, but future inhabitants in space could even start growing their own food while in orbit and eating fresh "locally grown" produce in the final frontier. (On a 2001 ISS mission, astronaut Susan Helms started growing a plant she found sprouting from an onion. She nurtured it with water and sunlight from a window on the orbiting laboratory.)

Take a "green" space tour from your backyard

One big reason to go into space is to see the stars without the haze or distortion in Earth's atmosphere. Smoggy glare is now in the skies over most cities and even the countryside. Going into Earth orbit gives you a better appreciation of our home in the universe. But there's another "green" way to see space, within a short drive! Astronomical societies have worked to set aside pockets of wilderness to be protected against light pollution. These areas are called dark sky preserves.

You can find your local dark sky preserve online by visiting websites such as www.wildernessastronomy.com. If you're interested, check out the nearest dark sky preserve and plan a "campsite astronomy" expedition with your family. No special equipment needed. Simply plan your route, pack your camping gear and supplies just as you would on any other trip and prepare to be amazed! You may have the chance to see a meteor shower, the northern lights and the Milky Way, part of our home galaxy. On a moonless night, you might even be able to read this book by the light of the Milky Way!

You'll also see spaceships in Earth orbit while camping. From satellites to the International Space Station, there are hundreds of human-made objects up there, some with people in them looking down at you right now. The orbits of human-inhabited vehicles are constantly changing, but you can find out which spacecraft will be flying over the dark sky preserve by using websites such as Heavens Above.

For example, here's how to find out when the ISS will pass over your house:
- Go to www.heavens-above.com/countries.aspx.
- Select your country. Then type the name of your town (or the one closest to you) into the "Search String" box.
- Click on your town, and you'll be taken to a page that lists many different satellites in orbit. Click on "ISS."
- You should now see a table with information on the dates during which you will be able to see the ISS. The table lists how bright the ISS will be using the magnitude scale (Mag). (A lower number means higher brightness: A bright star is 1 or 0, planets can be -2 or -3, and the full Moon is about -12.6). The table includes when the ISS will be at its highest point and when it will "set" on the horizon. The table will also show where the ISS will be in the sky (north, northwest, west northwest, etc.).

SPACE HOTELS

Up until now, the only place you'd see a space hotel is in a movie or a NASA concept painting. Such visions promised that hotels in space were right around the corner … 100 years or so from now.

But hotel entrepreneur Robert Bigelow didn't think that was good enough. The technology for space hotels already exists, and people are willing to pay for the service now. In 1999, Robert founded Bigelow Aerospace. He based his hotels on NASA's inflatable TransHab module technology, which he bought after the U.S. space agency canceled the TransHab program. Starting in 2006, Bigelow Aerospace launched a series of test hotels into orbit, the latest being one-third scale (large enough to host a convention of Hobbits, maybe).

The full-scale hotel modules will be made out of several layers of Vectran, a liquid crystal–based fiber twice as strong as Kevlar (the material bulletproof vests are made from). During launch, the modules are folded up in the nose of a rocket. Once they reach their destination, the module interiors are pumped with compressed air, inflating them to twice their original size. The inflation process for a one-third scale model takes about an hour.

Once the first full-sized test hotels with a human crew enter orbit, Bigelow hopes to offer four-week stays to the public by the end of 2012. The cost? US$15 million.

A more ambitious concept for a large space hotel involves launching many inflatable modules into orbit and connecting them by their rigid internal cores. A variation on this idea even includes a propulsion module to move the whole thing into orbit around our Moon or other planets.

An elevator to orbit

What's a hotel without an elevator? Right now, NASA and other space organizations are working with private companies to figure out how you might just ride a giant elevator into space. Such a highway to space would be made of advanced materials such as carbon nanotubes or even laser light. The journey would take longer than a rocket flight, but a space elevator would cut the cost of getting things into Earth orbit to a tiny fraction of the bill today.

Sound far-fetched? A NASA shuttle mission tested a cable of a few dozen meters in orbit on a mission in the 1980s. The experiment successfully showed that tethers in space can be deployed and kept tight for objects to travel along them. A later experiment successfully unraveled a 20 km (12 mi.) long test cable.

Such transportation systems would also mean you could get to your room in a space hotel more like you would in an Earthly retreat: Just hit the button for the 450 000th floor.

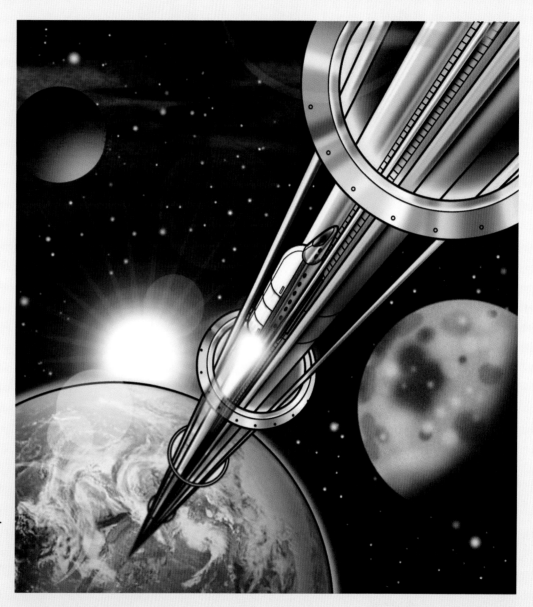

CONSTRUCTION AT 300 000 METERS

You might think that inflatable space modules would pop like a balloon, but they're actually even sturdier than rigid modules. That's because the strong materials they are made from are also flexible, so they can more easily absorb impacts from micrometeorites and other space debris.

Want proof? Blow up a balloon and tie it off in a knot. Then take a wooden kabob skewer and rub a little dish detergent on one of its sharp ends. Gently poke the balloon where it's darkest and thickest — opposite the knot. If you're careful, you can twist the point of your skewer "meteor" right through the balloon without popping it.

What's happening? Groups of molecules in the latex of the balloon are gently nudged aside by the pointy skewer. If the balloon were a more rigid structure of the same thickness, it would break apart. Full-scale inflatable habitats have some "give" in them compared to metal space modules.

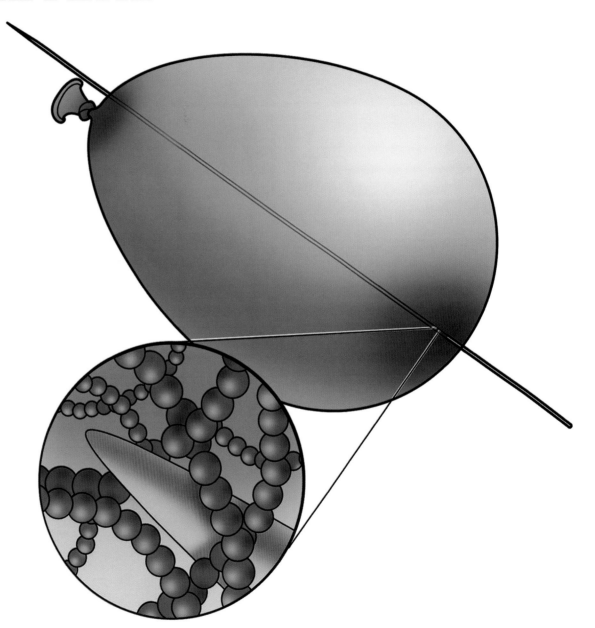

PROJECT #5: INFLATE A MODEL SPACE YACHT

One of the quickest ways to get hotels in space is to start with an orbital "yacht" and turn it into a sort of cruise ship in space. Such yachts could be built in orbit and grow to be larger than any ship that could be launched from Earth.

Author and NASA engineer John Spencer proposed that, as time went on, such yachts and super-yachts could become the in-between ships that carry tourists from Earth-launched space planes to monster-sized microgravity hotels.

He envisions space entertainment vehicles that could be launched folded up in a rocket and "unpacked" in orbit. In one version, a rigid core contains the vehicle's health care, storage,

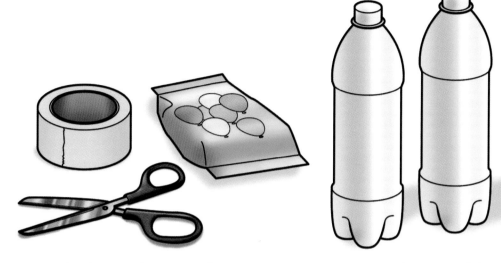

communications and command centers. Two inflatable modules would expand in orbit to make guest and crew cabins, as well as a dining area and observation deck. Part or all of these modules could be clear to serve as windows.

Want to see what one of these orbital yachts could look like? With an adult or friend to help, try your hand at making one in the following experiment.

YOU WILL NEED

two 500 mL (16 oz. or 20 oz.) plastic soda pop bottles

scissors

a roll of clear packing tape

a package of round party balloons

a friend or family member

Expert Interview

"The future of space hotels is definitely in inflatable structures. That's why the first version of an orbital yacht I designed, called *Destiny*, would mainly be built using inflatable modules. To see how we could transport such structures into space, construct the hard pop-bottle 'passageway' on the following pages and inflate its two habitation modules like the real thing."
— John Spencer, space architect

INSTRUCTIONS

1 Wash and dry your plastic bottles and remove any labels.

2 Cut the bottom off the first bottle at the point where the bottle widens to a consistent diameter. Cut the top off the second bottle, just where it starts to taper toward the bottle cap. The cut end of the second bottle should be slightly smaller than the cut end of the first bottle.

3 Insert the cut end of the second bottle into the cut end of the first bottle and secure with packing tape. IMPORTANT: The tape must form an airtight seal.

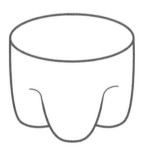

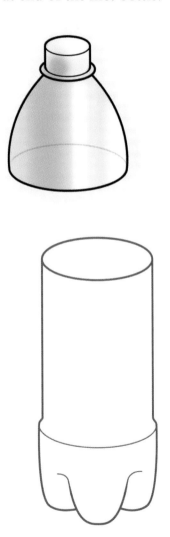

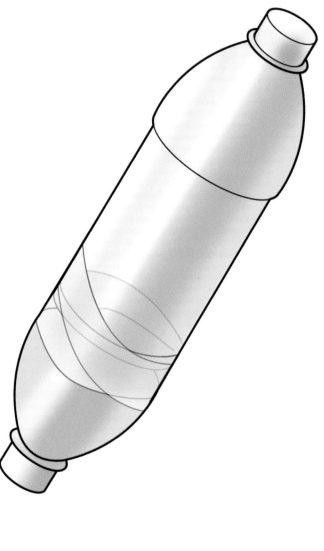

4 Unscrew one cap. Ask your helper to blow a balloon as big as possible and — without tying it — quickly place the nozzle of the balloon over the uncapped end of the plastic bottle assembly.

5 Ask your helper to quickly unscrew the remaining cap and tightly cover it with his or her hand. Blow up the second balloon and — as with the opposite end of the plastic bottle assembly — quickly place its nozzle over the remaining uncapped end.

6 Check for any leaks and quickly plug them with additional packing tape.

When you blow air from your lungs into the balloons, you are causing the balloons to expand by increasing the air pressure inside them. To achieve a similar effect, the rigid tunnel in the middle of inflatable space habitats will contain canisters of compressed air. When these are opened into the flexible parts of the structure, they will increase the air pressure, inflating a giant "balloon" that people can move around inside.

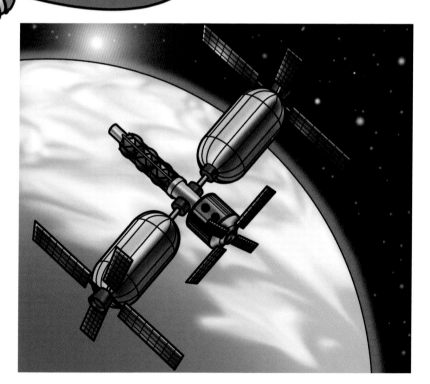

SOLAR SAILS AND RESORTS ON MARS

With regular flights to suborbital space already taking off and plans for hotels and cruise ships taking shape, what lies in the distant future of space tourism? Space pioneers are already eyeing the worlds beyond.

TO THE MOON!

There are many advantages to having a space base on solid ground instead of one that floats free in orbit. Several space agencies have plans to return humans to the Moon in the next few decades. (The last time we were there was 1972.) If enough people want to go, space tourism companies say a Moon hotel for entertainment might not be far behind. Imagine playing golf on the Sea of Tranquility or racing lunar rovers over the rim of a giant crater.

SOLAR SAILING

The technology already exists to "sail" on photons from the Sun. Gigantic sheets of paper-thin Mylar (the material used in welding glasses) can catch cosmic rays that would push a craft forward. A probe funded by members of The Planetary Society was set to demonstrate this technology in 2005, but the rocket carrying its *Cosmos 1* craft failed to get into space. The ship could have been the first large working solar sail in space — and the first successful space probe paid for by a special interest club.

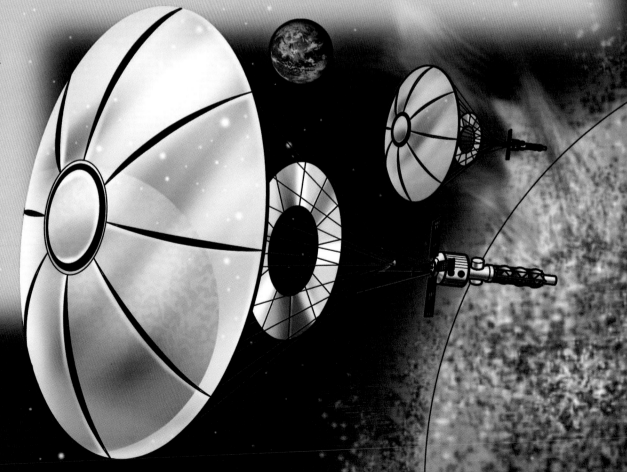

MARS

Trips into Earth orbit not exciting enough for you? How about a trip to the red planet? Several dozen times farther from Earth than the Moon, Mars has water, small amounts of Earth-like weather and a near-24-hour day. Imagine waking up to a pink-orange sky and red soil, seen through the windows of an inflatable habitat; hiking up the solar system's tallest mountain (Olympus Mons) and exploring the deepest, longest canyon known to humankind (the Mariner Valley).

TITAN

Saturn's super-moon is the second largest in the solar system. (It's larger than Pluto, about the size of Mercury and the only moon with a substantial atmosphere.) Because this moon contains liquid lakes and strong winds, it would actually be possible to enjoy a trip in an enclosed sailboat or even to windsurf in a special spacesuit.

TO THE STARS! THE DISTANT *DISTANT* FUTURE OF SPACE TOURISM

If we can vacation into suborbital space today and take trips to other worlds tomorrow, what fun could we have in space a hundred or more years from now?

Imagine vacationing on a giant donut-shaped space station so big that the inside of the station would have grassy valleys, low-gravity swimming pools and spaceship racing ports.

Imagine near-lightspeed ships taking families on day trips to the moons of the outer solar system, Pluto, Sedna and other distant ice worlds.

Imagine a faster-than-light space tourism vehicle that can take you into colorful clouds of stardust or to a planet orbiting another star like our Sun.

In the space vacation destinations of tomorrow, you could play sports in zero gravity, and then take a high-speed train to a rock-climbing expedition on another planet before enjoying dinner over the setting of an alien sun.

Where in the universe do *you* want to go on vacation?

Glossary

Atmosphere: the sphere-shaped envelope of gas surrounding planets like Earth. Humans going into space must take breathable atmosphere with them.

Eco-tourism: vacationing to ecologically interesting locations, with emphasis on preserving the natural environment

G-force: a force acting on a body (such as an astronaut) as a result of gravity or acceleration

Mass: the amount of matter in something: A massive planet has a lot more matter than a spaceship.

Module: a self-contained section of a structure, such as a space station or space hotel, that can be separated

Orbit: the curved path of a moon or spacecraft around another body such as a planet or star like our Sun

Probe: a human-made device that detects and measures. Space probes take scientific readings of conditions in space.

Satellite: an object that orbits around a planet, including natural satellites (moons and asteroids) and human-made ones (such as communications satellites and vehicles in orbit)

Simulation: an imitation to test something expected. Space simulations may imitate low gravity or extreme g-forces.

Space Tourist: someone who pays to go into space for fun or vacation, instead of going to space for work, such as for construction or exploration

Index